Night Became Years
Jason Stefanik

Coach House Books, Toronto

first edition

Published with the generous assistance of the Canada Council for the Arts and the Ontario Arts Council. Coach House Books also acknowledges the support of the Government of Canada through the Canada Book Fund and the Government of Ontario through the Ontario Book Publishing Tax Credit.

LIBRARY AND ARCHIVES CANADA CATALOGUING IN PUBLICATION

Stefanik, Jason, 1976-, author
Night became years / Jason Stefanik.

Poems.
Issued in print and electronic formats.
ISBN 978-1-55245-363-6 (softcover).

I. Title.

PS8637.T433N54 2018   C811'.6   C2018-900931-4
                                                  C2018-900932-2

Night Became Years is available as an ebook: ISBN 978 1 77056 540 1 (EPUB) ISBN 978 1 77056 543 2 (PDF)

Purchase of the print version of this book entitles you to a free digital copy. To claim your ebook of this title, please email sales@chbooks.com with proof of purchase. (Coach House Books reserves the right to terminate the free digital download offer at any time.)

Table of Contents

Before I present the reader with the following primer of Beggars Cant, I think it not amiss to premise with a few words on the nature of Beggars themselves, by way of historical consideration, of the antiquity of the former and the universality of the latter: for though Beggars are found in all countries alike, they are not in all countries alike, their nature and genius being diverse in proportion to the countries in which they stroll, as now it is affirmed that they effect equally the countries where they rose and of those through which they pass.

– A New Dictionary of the terms Ancient and Modern of the Canting Crew, In its Several Tribes, of Gypsies, Beggars, Thieves, Cheats, &c., by B. E. Gent

Strowlers, c. Vagabonds, Itinerates, Men of no settled abode, of a precarious life. Wanders of Fortune, such as Gypsies, Beggars, Peddlers, Hawkers, Mountebanks, Fidlers, Country-Players, Rope dancers, Juglers, Tumblers, showers of Tricks, and Raree-show-men.

Sleepwalking

Never are your nights this long, body entombed
with exhaustion, mind ensnared in a mesh
of pixels and elusive pinwheels of REM.

In the pleasant ether of neither-nor, with sleeplessness
past your book's yellowing font, your dust
and rancour of lust and conflict,

and the nauseous popple of sleeping pills, to a space
where darks are deeply black, lights deeply bright,
and you're ardent in the gills of your distant past.

A madrigal hummed by a mummer choir
mimics the lapping of waves on sunken
blocks of limestone. With an acorn under your tongue,

you watch backyards careen across the rungs
of oily current. You're holding on, encouraging
an unstudied, somatic dull, for you feel

the night is special, feel the compulsion
to prolong your dream the duration
a daemon can possess a candle flame.

Travel Advisory

Don't come. The pictures are fake,
Photoshopped stock foliage. This is the land
of the ruthless usurper. It's hard to crowbar away
the hooded upstart jimmying the bathroom window.
I live here, don't come. I've murderous nieces
I've not yet met. A whole birth family, social workers say,

who're bikers, boozers, free-basers, bums. Even Mom,
I'm told, drinks away our taxes in a lakeside teepee.
If you come, someone will smash a window of your camper van.
If you stay too long, your nights will lengthen with pain
like a housecoated family watching their home burn.
You may feel the touch of love, yes, temporarily,

but by dawn you're found hog-tied in a garage.
Neighbours suspect it's drug related. When news breaks
you're also in a cult of FAS, the cops
downgrade the case. How tauntingly severe is this place
when you come – we're hand in hand down the lane,
wind taking us toward the searing white sun.

Unfortunate Traveller

Unfortunate Traveller, where have you been?
I've known a chunky kid with humped back,
laggard and ah-shucks shy, shuffling
amid a gang zone while intoning a psalm.

Unfortunate Traveller, what have you heard?
I've heard the whispers of children in the aisles
while they discuss the crowded plight of the crabs
bound by rubber bands in the tank at Superstore.

Unfortunate Traveller, how does it feel?
It feels like booths of widows and widowers
swallowing their life's pain with red velvet cake
in the stale light of a late-night dinette.

Unfortunate Traveller, were your senses keen?
They divined the old cat who doesn't want
to see you cry, who won't meet your eye
before you take her to the vet to get put down.

Unfortunate Traveller, how deep the seeing?
I saw the love as a girlfriend recalled James, dead
this year of AIDS, and who, though a bullied gay boy,
asked her as his date to their high school grad.

Unfortunate Traveller, did you find the way?
I came to starlings in a thorn bush, asleep
by an airport fence, watched sun-vaulting silverfish
blazing atop the wave tips at Winnipeg Beach.

Unfortunate Traveller, what did the signs say?
They showed a small girl still pure enough to ride tall
on the back of her mom's wheelchair through the mall,
their faces twinned with love as they dodge and palter.

Unfortunate Traveller, where did you stay?
In an ice-fishing shack with some rough farm kids – glad
they traded in their shit-kicking boots for a pack
of Zig-Zags – using Red River jigs to fiddle and fish.

You turn off at an unfamiliar bend of road.
Silence is not forgiveness but stupefaction,
like an essay dug out of a messy desk
before a snide teacher and unfriendly class.

Grief Like the Night

I know, another poem about rape
in our small town, but in school they're talking
about a rape at a bush party this past Friday
where the accused are cousins of the reeve.

No poem captures grief like the night
we heard about a sister's stiffened corpse.
She had tried crossing, without shoes or clothing,
frozen fields to the offices of Public Works.

About her, in shop class, we said it wasn't
quite rape, per se, but more a property crime.
A pimp-drug-dealer had traded her in
for a wide-tank hog in need of new paint.

Every girl knows about the warming shack
beside the hockey rink, the hunting camp
with tourist dollars – where no sex offence
ends in charges. This latest rape, forget it.

No level of policing will care one bit.
Our teacher said the girl blacked out by the pond,
when two bros she'd hung with since she was a kid
told her, 'Lift your shirt, let us feel those tits.'

Swig-men, c. the 13th Rank of the Canting Crew, carrying small Habberdashery-Wares about, pretending to sell them, to colour their Roguery.

Advent

I'll follow you
to the heat-lamp diner.
Follow you
to the fruitfly barstool.
Follow you
over wailing overpasses.
Follow you
to bedbug theatres.
Follow you
down warehouse elevators.
Follow you
into communal gardens.
Follow you
to where, with disinterest,
we can wallow
amid the gristle
of food-court cynics.
Follow you
to visit a keen-eyed Inuk
under a crumbling icebridge
where we can kiss.
We're nine grandmothers
removed from nomads,
with nine beautiful sisters
to teach us numbers.
I'll follow you.

Aphorisms of a Visored Paladin

At some point you'll finally feel the old show's double entendre dull
in a hyper-sexualized world.

When the greenery was haranguing you into joining it for spring,
shouldn't you have plied a trade?

If your eyes past midnight bled with metaphor and effort,
good.

The cat you passed up forever tingled behind
like a war vet's ghost limb.

Why didn't you, Steven, Bank Manager, friend, say life was a roll
of receipts tallying from first credit card to below the grass?

Those molten burps bursting in your throat never heralded
the brouhaha before the heart attack.

She was a Cree scoutress, quiet through wood, ear to ground,
and I lost her trail.

You know you raved too hard those two years in a row the Best Cheddar
    in the British Empire
went to Bothwell.

So you didn't make the NHL – weren't you a foot-hockey champion, who
    pounded home
a frozen tennis ball at the backstop mesh when high up slot?

You know the man of eighty-something highlighting his Bible beside you
was you.

The hoebag devouring pomegranates in the nightshower was you.

Since he was one serious imam, you were one serious Orangeman when
    you were drunk.

The mucked-up world, when a high school English teacher informed
the only people reading it are poets.

An acid-wash jean jacket with *Anarchy* felt-markered black
on the back is not that bad after all.

Rejoice for all the years Astrology.com sent you a birthday card.

Thank God you pulled out when your diet fell to hell,
Cantonese and creatine by the bellyful.

Hemmed in the indigo gloam of a basement bedroom, more like a bordello
of velvet black drapes, us trinity of Goth kids, so far gone into Dungeons
    and Dragons,
rolled out our fates on twenty-sided die, and you, Steven, Bank Manager,
    friend,
were always the DM.

Sister Aspires to Destress

Sister got sloppy on Oxycontin.
It really set our broken home into motion.
Her basement teen-den decompressed one afternoon
Sister and her bestie rolled a Shoppers.
I didn't agree with Mom enrolling me in martial arts
when she was overcome with unspeakable woe
and signed me on for classes in tae kwon do.

I didn't want to live, so what the hell:
I wanted to go and beat someone down.
I wanted to be someone beaten down.
Dad hated me for not writing to him in jail. I hated
him for not escaping to kill Stepdad. Alphonse!

Sister got floppy on Oxycontin
and I was gifted a white belt and crackling white gi.
All credit to me, I snuck from the school library
a dog-eared tome on *Jeet Kune Do* by Bruce Lee
and spent hours each night throwing daggers
at a backyard tree. To prep for the Tuesday I'd arrive
at the dojo on my blue ten-speed Raleigh.

Street-fighting, Master said, was the class's emphasis.
Striking pressure points, gouging eyes, kneeing groins
was the best defence, and in twenty minutes
my ribs cracked holding pads for the Master's son.
He beat me to tears in the sparring session.
I yearned for a hole to fill up inside me,
unlike Sister. She aspired to empty.

Night Caprice

The blend of humour
and humiliation, Tina,
when I saw you sitting
on another man's lap.
The feeling of élan!
To finally solve your lost pounds,
your trumping our every debate
with last words. Hooray, night caprice,
hooray, pyjamas furnaced
to my epidermis. Hooray, lust
conspiring that bid me
overcome my whispering
woes and taxi to your place.
I can now puzzle out
the night I heard for minutes
when you pocket-dialled me
from your purse, and you laughed
happier than I'd heard in months.
At last I know without wishing
to know, and it soothes me some:
you keep me at the edge of town
for when you're older, uglier,
and need to settle down.

Talking Shit

How you hold such unflinching love for him – you can't
know him as I've known him. A bony kid too sickly

to lug his tuba home to practice. A jazz improviser
awaiting only a single treacherous chance.

An exasperator, a sluffer, sulking in the hull
rather than earning keep pulling lobster traps.

A pimply line cook huffing nitrous from Whip-It cans.
A reeling religious erratic who fails to rouse

his drunken uncles for midnight mass. An oily oldie,
with the same pesky authority as a game-show host,

insisting mumbly kids elocute their responses.
A dirty letch, double-yoked by mere chance, to the coax

of any pheromone-sticky tongue. A career sellout
claiming he's writing the comedies our city requires.

A dull consignment and I'll-convert-on-my-deathbed optimist.
A flophouse violinist in flip-flops on social assistance.

A lisping DJ on public radio with an itch for 'S' titled songs.
A boy wanker busted by camera-savvy buddies

between crooked venetian slats. A third-liner at best
afraid of going in the corners and taking a hit.

The type of tweaker who couldn't last one hour
within the Pen's general population, and I wager

when you hear of him again he's already dead
and I'm a full-patched Sergeant of Arms in the gang.

Cousin Ass at Bingo

Orst wraggles the hush at late-night bingo.
I hate the Ass. Whereas rows of quainter fogies
wear bifocals and blink at the number board,
Orst wears wrap-around shades, earbuds abuzz
with Frankie Yankovic and the Polka Kings.
He and I share the same wobbly table,

dabbing two cards apiece. I despise
the way waitresses avoid us, mostly Orst,
as they shirk bringing peanuts for his leering
up their skirts. His meat hook rarely cups
a buttock without a prong toward the pelvis.
His bombast snarls across the dulcet

professional tones of ushers inspecting cards.
The Spaniard in the money cage, he cusses
for peeping at a paperback while not on break.
Over and over, Orst tells of the afternoon
he laid the beats to a gangbanging kid
for barring the path to a beer fridge.

'That's nothing compared to the May Long
I brawled both LeValley boys and a junkie
Eskimo behind McLaren Hotel,' boasts Orst.
I loathe the Ass until the vodka shots dry out
his tongue. When he passes out, pisses himself,
and I cuff a ten-spot from his wallet.

Real Estate Ballad

Resale is guaranteed in that precision:
the curb sits higher than the snowplough's grade.
Barely a busted trough along the roofline:
I judge the builder by how the basement's laid.
How fierce the family dog needing shade
depends whether the garden shed's breached;
I know the buyer by the down payment paid:
it's on a great piece of land – motion cams are cheap.

I merit the neighbour by his friendly strut
and see a cat that is not an alley cat;
single from married moms I can tell apart:
foul kid from holy I divine by the tat.
Keep the door unlocked, but sleep with a bat;
nobody clears the back fence in a leap.
Down the street there's a coin-op laundromat,
it's on a great piece of land – leg traps are cheap.

I tell the truth for each property I list,
whether the seller asks for it or not:
I point to flaws other agents missed,
like how at the stoop a kid's cat got shot.
I know the convict by the time he's got;
but moms dream well if they knit before sleep.
No graffiti artist here will get caught,
it's on a great piece of land – bleach is cheap.

Friend, for the cost of a paid tithe, own this land;
walk with your son to where the food bank's deep,
all the opportunity you ever dreamed,
it's on a great piece of land – deadbolts are cheap.

Palliards, c. the seaventh rank of the Canting Crew, whose Fathers were Born Beggars, and who themselves follow the same Trade, with Sham Sores, making a hideous Noise, Pretending grievous Pain, do exhort Charity.

Hunting Grounds

From out of a frost-mottled scarf, I hear Michif
when not in the Sally Ann. For warmth I flex
my tendons under thrift-store layers, and loiter
as long as I can in any gas station washroom.
I make jobs, collect cans. I keep my boots slogging
a salty grocery cart. For one heel of day-old bread
I barter to thaw in a ATM. I rebirth

two rag-and-bone men from a snowbank, surveying
the virtue of their hand-me-downs: fusty folds
of grunge cardigans, oversized sweats, and clashing plaids.
Their same self-medicated mumblecore I recognize.
We form a party to attack the corroded bicycle padlocked
to a church fence. We're undeterred by the slow pass
of police. We batten and bilk with snickery gibberish

at the Gospel Union Outreach Wagon, and absorb
flashlight probing for coffee and beef broth
from med-school undergrads. Off the overpass,
we bivouac in the rivets of an industrial park,
where we can pull off our balaclavas and squat
beside the grates blowing hot factory air, to share
our fresh cuts of dog tail roasted over paint can.

Scanterbury Church

Wind will compound to blanch fields as bone;
twilight bleeds now like hamstrung venison.
A lakeside sharpens into jagged stone
that can cut a hoof, but nothing crosses here
where kin dissolves into chalk-dry overtone.
Who is a symmetry without bearing –
we've backed the liars, everything will perish.
Before and after this world, we're alone,
while all fails from birth canal to casket.

Sun and snow will crystal-film as one.
On steeple and headstone, frost catches shine.
Who knows when the last parishioner came
to slouch at a pew in doleful antiphon,
to hear the wind beat through the rickety gate
like a skull shrieking blasphemies, and sense
coffins cracked apart by shifts of ground.
With sulphurous rankling and without love, we run
from the light of day to the dark we fell from.

Nine Texts from the Toronto Hyatt

Stereo dot scuds,
wince below ear point – just.
My Cameo singe winks
on the mattress scalped pink.
Will the housemaid guess?

Clattery guts fridge
whose histrionic insides
seal hooch in the head.
I cipher over ice
on my room charges.

No porter would guess
my tread in the fit station
in not-so-roomy Spandex,
with giblets brimmed,
I timed my best.

Pull-tab cheese slices
scarfed from polymer sleeves,
my pleasant supper
guests compared to Newfie
oilmen wanting weed.

Snazzier hotel;
dimmer tubes of light below.
Chromatic ice machine,
the Roboguard down the hall,
doles my hooch coolant.

Would the valet guess
if I press her a fiver,
say of a Lexus,
'Please keep an eye on 'er,'
I just can't take the bus?

The broomball team up the hall
dehydrates the ice machine.
Its musical doors,
with marital intrigues,
peepholing my dreams.

Spy a night audit
deploy her Congolese wit
to diffuse a fight
between rival husbands
vying for Captain.

Four hours till late checkout.
The crystal ledgers waver
like a dimensional incident,
trapped over bilge-water fog,
and buses nowhere at this hour.

Dada Is an Alpha Male

Dada plays in a dart league, a shuffleboard league,
a few curling bonspiels. He puts in long days
without lunches, yet he's never one to dither on
about how drone-like is his life. Guys out drinking
during the weekends admire him watching porn

with his new wife. 'I love gingerbread,' he says;
'I don't, I hate it,' she says, but they get along nice.
Throughout the poplar-boxed neighbourhood
for sure he knows his is the restored muscle car
with the most balls. He polishes it Sundays

on the drive wearing earbuds and short-shorts.
Twice now he's pried himself free from families
with affairs, but I give him credit that he manages
and even surpasses the heft of his child support
by winning the bids for government tenders.

Complex man, you bet, he started to read books
and thinks my teacher is stupid for not teaching us
the poems of Carl Sandburg. My Dada is so ripped,
rich, smart, ready to drive around me and my friends,
I don't know how I'll admit to my latest mom, I heard
Dada bragging about a sitter blowing him.

Brandy Doesn't Love Me

Brandy was her name and she was a widow
to a long-haul trucker. She was a coy brunette

who would go to the bar in her Daisy-Dukes,
and she kept her call-tag active, *Tosh's Belle*,

by the time I met her smoking her menthol smokes.
Her turkey neck she hated, but she paid

off her house, and her pastel bangles, jumpsuits,
and knack with casseroles drew me in

to the triangles of her tanlines and bones –
plus her way of basement slow-dancing me

to Lionel Richie and Boney M, interrogating me
on whether I make eyes at any cheerleaders.

Now I work the night shift at a hot dog cart.
Tosh's Belle replaced me. I skry her dark fringe

at the register of the dinette, or in the gloss
across the aisle with the Dollar Tree's mop.

By her fondue, painting her toenails barium blue,
half-done the last chapter of a Harlequin,

and I see Tosh pulling out the drive with his rig
a last time. Even though I know she loves

the love letters I forge for Tosh and leave
in her mailbox, it's hurtful she's involved police.

Bro Code

All taxi drivers despise me –
they hate my bros showing deltoids
in muscle shirts and loose chains;
they hate when we request louder tunes,

when we ask to light up just one smoke,
if we can still stop at some place
this late to buy booze. They hate
us trying to schmooze off-meter,

asking how fare the kids and wife
all the way back home overseas.
We ruin women with lust, they insist,
their statues on their dashboards –

it's a matter of fact some suffer
no wrong turns, study the cosmos,
and suggest we're asses braying
at the gravity of our morality.

Yet isn't this Saturday night fresh
with ravishment – isn't there yet
festivity in this, good coachman?
They hate us when we tip them big,

especially if we didn't know
where we're going, or why
we insist they shake our hands,
hug them close and call them bros.

Tramp Camp

Though gentrification and crack bullies inhabit
most vacant inner-city houses where you can squat,
a lucky ramble into the outskirts can procure
your holiday retreat from the streets. Put on your best
clothes and recce during daylight hours: at night

you not only set off alarm bells but can't dissemble
earmarks of an empty shell. Gardens grown to bramble
or bracken, power or water meters at zero, broken
windows or door hinges – look close and you'll discern
where owners have left you their premises.

Once established, move in, recalling less force means
less chance of a charge for break-and-enter. Just an owner,
or an owner's agent, can evict you (like a shelter),
so don't feel threatened if you're spotted by neighbours –
if you're respectful they may even help you.

Cherish the experience as long as it lasts. You can
dust, try your hand at fixing floorboards, chase away
feral cats, or jerk off in peace. While reclining,
hearken back to when you were a kid at Christmas,
still rich with the confidence for living-room vaudeville.

Abram-men, c. the seventeenth Order of the Canting-crew. Beggars antickly trick'd up with Ribbands, Red Tape, Foxtails, Rags, &c. pretending Madness to palliate their Thefts of Poultrey, Linnen, &c..

To Realize Your Love

I'd transcend the smokestacks in their nests,
stanch with salt my paper cuts,
cross a steppe with but a gunny sack,
nail an ace on my physics test,
mug a tosser at the horse track,
and take a volley in the artillery butts,
I would.

To realize your love
I'd ignore a stranger in a dream,
surpass a suggested gratuity,
break free from a Scientology compound,
squint at the snow in a moonbeam,
learn the hymns of Moody and Sankey,
and flip a junebug tipped on the ground,
I could.

To realize your love
I'd shrimp a pearl from an octopus's tooth,
bake an eel pie on a kelp stove's flue,
be the old dog backed over on the drive,
confront a mullah with a backpack nuke,
press that the Waldensian screed revive,
and cash in my carbon credit for you,
I should.

Night Skating

Frozen river, night skating watched from my balcony
with the volatility I've come to link
as yours: without requiring as much as one spark
but bounding up out of black while gliding on ice.

Time crackles out of a loudspeaker to remind you
it's last skate. You catch something of your fate in the immense
and dark fields, the fragility of memory moving
down river, skating backward, revealing ice.

As now after ploughing, two white prehistoric spines
pushing northward to the Thompson Nickel Mines.
I can't unpuzzle your silhouette from the sticks,
just unanswering black down the path of ice.

Nothing spotted for countless intervals, countless heartbeats,
but I may have caught the wattage of your mercurial blades,
or the soft far-off explosions of blasting caps
in the open-pit mines procuring precious ore.

Crown Defence

There is a teacup trembling away on the landing.
You crack open the door and the parents are fighting

as you enter the cabin. All the fathers are standing
with your own father trying to play peacemaker –

but this is unacceptable to your mother's friends,
as everyone – not including your favourite uncle –

considers your father a drunken scoundrel.
Then he reaches in his vest for the knife he carries.

You tell Child Services you don't know what happened.
Down the hallway you hear the caseworker whisper,

there were some she could help and some she couldn't.
Imagine your decision if this was your upbringing.

Fortune

Fortune, what a strange bedfellow
you make, wanting you to lie
closer when I desire some
of your alms: rattling devil's bones

between my palms,
never mind lucky sevens, but double sixes
or a snake eyes, I'm addicted
to your replicating kisses.

When I think I'm winning, like a champ
tetherballer on a playground,
Fortune, soon by you I'm bound,
and *vodka* is my safe word.

Slag

My butch cousin doffs a smoke at the steel mill.
Out by the trash bins and piss-stained snowbanks,
my butch cousin hams in her best punch-drunk,
thick vowels and phantom consonants:
'I'm not worried about airborne AIDS.'

'Look at the fucking landscape,' she burps.
'You think this is peach-and-gold-coloured
like a French whorehouse, I see one bird,
a plain oriole on the rail fence, and each winter
fender-benders burst into gunfights.'

She hoofs the STOP sign: Nothing matters,
she'll never stay caught in some warm, well-lined nest.
'Look at the sign above the slag heap,' she snorts,
'Clean Fill Wanted, isn't that the story of our lives.'
Our smoke break is about done, anyways.

Intervention

Beth was a big-boned girl who touched off with her Ouija board
a rural-town chain of suicides. Dawn and Lisa joined Beth,

starting with Bloody Mary in the hermetic, dark,
unfinished basement bathroom, twirling in pink tank tops

and pyjama bottoms toward the mirror. 'I saw her red fangs,'
squealed Dawn, swearing later to the Lord she wasn't pushing

as the planchette spoke with Marilyn Monroe. 'Well, Norma Jean,
since she likely resumed her original name,' said Dawn,

and the next day they found Dawn, hung from a jungle gym, dead.
Lisa used one finger when she and Beth spoke with Chad Brown,

a kid from her old school who drowned on a field trip to the pool,
and Lisa said she suspected someone held him down, now

she knew, it was the East Indian boy who loved Chad's girl.
For some reason, the day after Dawn's funeral, Lisa

pedalled her bike into the light of an oncoming train.
From that day, for Beth, nothing was the same. In the next weeks

there were police, grief counsellors, a professed ex-Wiccan priestess
for the occult intervention, though no matter how many tapered

black candles and incense sticks her parents could confiscate,
Beth sat with her body language clenched, preening her bangs

into her view while buck-toothing her lip ring. Then Beth met Bob,
an older man who owned the town's empire of hot-dog carts,

both living in complete bliss till the steel-mill layoffs, and cash-poor Bob slit his wrists for his compounded debts, when Beth

put a gun barrel up her mouth. Since the day Beth asked guidance from her planchette, invisible dark hands pushed her to the end.

Today she rooms with a sawbones in a tarpaper shack.

Patricio, or c. Pater-cove, c. the Fifteenth Rank of the Canting Tribe, stroling Priests that Marry under a Hedge without Gospel or Common-prayer Book, the Couple standing on each side a Dead Beast, are bid to Live together till Death them do's Part, so shaking Hands, the Wedding is ended; also any Minister, or Parson.

Muscle Memory

I can't guess, Tina, what you think. Can't guess what we'll do next.
Think I know it's nothing. Now you're in the South of France
downloading my email to your PalmPilot.

My reply to your wry, unsigned hoof-you-in-the-gut
e-postcard of a grain elevator getting off in August
nowhere near Marseille.

Fourteen times, the behaviourists say, to condition a human.
You can feel our muscle memory break down, I'm sure.
The change in field from where we are today,

so far we've come, from 7-Eleven under awning, green halogen.
Kinda nerds. Your crotch of bubblegum jeans a hot-spurred V
at my hip, while we gargled Fizz Pop,

our Slurpees hyped with vodka hops, and petting limits
in public places, those kerchiefed Marseillians
never dreamed or downloaded.

When it nearly started, when we were young
but hooded-up kids, straight from date site to chatline,
off to warehouse roller rink,

raving hard till the sunny-sides at truck-stop dinettes.
Time and space of such dingy and less dignified public places,
than canopied cafes with decanters of aperitif.

Nowhere near where we are today, where our muscle memory
can't feel for what's ahead. Here comes my unsigned e-postcard
of bleached white cliffs embossing Dover Beach.

Gaming Commission

Inner-city bingo hall, chinchilla mink abounds.
With the sisters of the Willow Goddess, we chase
the crier in an X-pattern with soft daubs. How hapless
the mumbling that snakes the tinsel banners, suppresses
our doubtful looks while an usher audits a card.

Never hers. Never mine. In a hoar-crusted
modular transit shed, our faces stalled
with hypostasis off the tundra wind,
our ghostwriting eyes behind oversized shades,
our mood's anemic blue. Until we're back in our room,

back home without any pentacles in our lives,
snared by the royal bondage of our loss,
as the whip kisses x x x 's down the length of the spine,
saying, 'Mea culpa, we chase clean lucre for once,
fuck you, Matthew Arnold, oh fuck you.'

Orst at Wedding Socials

Don't let his paisley baby-blue suit fool you
    or get tricked by the sophisticated tint
of his Wayfarers – when Cousin Orst flashes cufflinks,
    you should know by the time the cops show
he'll confirm why everyone hates him.
    You'll see the teary-eyed bride pleading in a mic
for everyone to pipe down, but everyone will guess

    she means Orst, the doltish brute I'm stuck beside,
always driving around with his crewcut buddies,
    as they pick fights and pretend they're ignorant
to kindness of others with their deranged squints.
    They're the dicks at the door without any tickets,
so don't pretend you won't see it happening;
    Orst never tires of demanding for a man

to hit him first. You may espy his coiffed shine
    with peeping watch chain, or the turquoise cross
in his tufting chest hair, but when the emcee blares
    'I Knew the Bride When She used to Rock 'n' Roll,'
he'll stare out in the Quaalude delirium
    of George Jones shifting gears. As lights flick on
you'll witness the silvery jughead looping

    hammerfists (naked of his rhinestone blazer,
in just a bloody wifebeater on the dance floor)
    to prove he's still the bull's horns at sixty-four.
But when he outruns the sirens later,
    and we're behind his shed, hidden in the pines,
when he hugs me and tells me nobody loves him,
    the blubbery crybaby I can't help but hold.

Visiting Cross Lake

A linchpin pulled from the temperate. Winter detonated
like an upturned snowglobe. I can't tip my visor in crazed adoration,
but I'm giddy at the prospect of love with her again.

Today I feel forgiven, the dross washed from my Cossack
atrocities; I feel the cold reverb of autumn deepen
with a numbing, humbling assonance of northwind.

Her favour I'll prescribe as holy, and prove by deeds
her deification; her presence I'll meet on a bowed knee
before my sudden erasure in a snowstorm.

Hard

Practically a single mom.
My baby's daddy is basically a bum,
without any beer or time to chip in.
I wish he'd pull before he comes.

I was a hot girl in tight white pants behind the mall
eating Tiger-Tiger ice cream.
If he wasn't such a pussy he'd try his hand at crime,
but my baby's daddy is not the kind

who could spend time in the Pen.
When he goes for smokes he'd better run –
if they catch him on the corner they're going to roll him
for the meth they loaned his hoodlum mom.

I wish he wouldn't let our son hold his gun.
I can't wait to get drunk after the baby is born.
He took our money for diapers and Pablum
and put it on Pro-Line. Our living room coffee table

he put into pawn. He could never get a loan,
and that pay-as-you-go-phone, he never turns on.
He says he'll slap me when he doesn't like my tone,
but I could boot his scrawny ass back to Pukatawagan.

Resource Rights

I date a hot Inuit gal from Tuk
and I hate how she dates a porter
named Coco at a remote lake

the summers she caters
for nickel prospectors. She's tricked
by Coco and his Bible sermons,

his dark rum, his slippery prophecies,
his maudlin trapline blessings,
how – his latest – he talked down

a kid with FAS who stole a paddle
and killed another kid's dad.
In town she avoids me, and should

I track her, she says I don't know
about rapture, no chance I limbo
as low as her Coco.

I've heard German engineers,
core-sampling for Schlumberger,
get friendly with her, once

she met with a Mexican
custodial night crew
contracted by Talisman.

If I could get her sober, I should
tell her I talked to a pastor.
I pray she forgets Coco,

but in case I can't reach her
I'll appeal to the Crown
to demand she settle down.

For Marina Tsvetaeva

Foreknow the night,
my honeyed dram,
that black chert
and clay bank.
To the hairpins
and resplendent narcotic
of your jewels
I smile inward salutes,
so nice to be offsite
for four days.

Our altar is earth
and mankind sacrifice
while the union turns
scabrous: building Hydro Pole
Two, those big-talkers
are always the biggest
dog-fuckers, the stewards
infest the ears
of management, the foreman –

'Hullo there! Piss on him!'
Darling Marina,
how do we interrupt
you roping your baby
to a booster seat
so you could go eat
with your eldest son? Mamma,
tell us about Water Babies,
the seashore dream
and shadow of Poseidon
at the great dam.

The Vengeance of Cutwolfe

I could not prepare for the incident thrust upon
the night I squared up at the pub and crossed the rail yards.
How wonderfully strange, the Lord's judgments.

Through a chink in a rail shed I could see the back
of his body, his arms lashed to a lawnchair, his breath
condensing by a hung bulb. Figures circled him.

A green rubber glove clutched a hatchet. The Lord
may've watched when he confessed his name, Cutwolfe,
and then began to utter his oration.

'Though you heathens sit and hope to see my liver slit,
my teeth plied out for tooth soup, my body
broken with slavish repentance, you'll not hear

such beggary from me. With tongue intact I confess
myself murderous. Pain cannot afflict remorse:
I'm the champion who slew Dubois, the Emperor

of Homicides, two years to the day he slew my brother
on a dock in Traverse Bay, and this opiates my nerve endings. He,
from the faraway diocese of Duck Lake,

who slew my oldest and gentlest brother
over a wretched woman, giddily I avenged myself on,
suturing my nerve endings from your torture.

News of Brother came as my family trolled the shore,
and Mother's wailing barbed like tackle in my eardrums.
Father granted me permission to sell our boat and netting,

and turn our fishing licence in for the funding,
to scourge after Dubois with a club and pistol.
For twenty-four months, I pursued the butcher, from Peguis

to Roseau Rapids, from Riding Mountain to Lizard Point,
then across the lake at Seekaskootch and back
toward Peguis where I heard he was attending

Pow Wow Days in Brokenhead. While I waited I fed
on gooseberries and wild carrot. In tall oat grass I dreamt
and can't recall what pursuits I followed, so overcome

was I for the time that dog would take the fairgrounds.
Brave young men fled like bison when it was confirmed
the notable assassin from Duck Bay arrived.

With his disciples around I would not challenge
him to duel, but waited to exploit every advantage,
tracking him riverside where he squatted in a hovel.

When I entered he demanded that I state my errand.
"This," I snarled. "Dubois, the nasty backstabber
of Duck Bay – my oldest brother you gutted dockside

during Treaty Days, and two years since
I've hounded you three thousand miles for revenge.
If I felt my vengeance flagging, I'd recall Mother

yanking out her hair, shrieking, wailing, and Father
crawling on his hands in pain along the cold sand.
Now I face you, at the mercy of my power, and promise

the devil will own your soul within an hour.
Don't squirm, don't flinch, I've a gold-capped bullet
blessed by every auntie to bury in your breast."

But your friend, Dubois, he was a beggar till his last words.
He pleaded, "I have quillwork fineries. I have uncut beryl
hid in a birch tree's hollow whorl.

Inflict me with punishment. Barb hooks through my eyelids,
force me to stare into northwind off an icebound lake.
For harming your brother, the festering rot

of my brains, I must suggest, is punishment enough.
No hell is hotter than the burning spear of my thoughts
since the night judgment slipped and I jabbed at your brother.

For the betterment of my soul, I beg, allow my body
to live on tormented: spoon out my eyes, spade out my ears,
carve away my tongue and nose that I may think awhile.

I can teach you: man is only his thought. To live, walk,
dream each second leavened with burdensome murdering,
erodes a man into unspeakable evil acts.

Stay your hand from liberating my villainous mind.
I am not tamed, for yesterday passing through Batoche
I attacked the husband of a woman who gawked at me.

The terror of your arrival lit a kingdom of possibility
in my coal heart, and the instant fear of my own death
can serve a higher purpose than your limiting stroke.

You pursued these terrible miles because your heart
was petrified, and yet it was not you I injured, let you
and I cleanse this cyclical violence from our history.

Finally, if you dispatch me from my torment, I can't pray
for your immaculate soul, that it may release from the mire
that I've bubbled within you by no fault of your own."

Eagerly I replied to his bullshit speechcraft.
"Though I know the Lord shall have no mercy,
except what I show on you, for you I'll spare

not a smidge. Revenge in our daily events
is wrought from hell. Hell I esteem better than heaven
as it grants revenge, for no heaven exists save revenge.

For heaven's bliss I would not undertake such toiling
as done to exploit you for revenge. Divine revenge! Look,
my shins are splintered to limping from tailing your path.

I have wracked my throat's lining in howling curses.
I have ground my teeth to powder from hearing your name.
My eyes disconnected, bloodied, with charting your trail,

as I envisioned plans when I finally captured you.
Pretending they were you, I scalped trees in the forest,
so determined was I to execute my purpose.

Snivel not, you'll not know the grace of a divine miracle,
only this blade rending your sulphuric entrails."
But your clansman begged for me to spare his blood.

He whimpered. "Hold. Wait. Hear this tempting proposal out.
Since you care not for God, and aim your volition whole
on vengeance, consider how you can best exploit this

by making me pervert the testaments of Christendom.
I'll cut the throats of my kindred. I'll burn men, women,
and children in their beds. I'll break each Lord's Commandment

each hour of the day, and I'll gut pious confessors
disguised in priest robes. In your merciful name I'll renounce
my baptismal, with any interest I still retain

in holy sacraments. I can serve as lieutenant
to your vicious precepts if only you would relent
your hand for the opportunity I'm offering."

At his vile skullduggery I smiled, somewhat,
not in reversal of my resolve, but compounded
in my forces to debase him double: my mind travelled

in quest of some new clever marvel with wide platform
to not only destroy his body, but the core of his soul.
The basis was this: for the sake of me, he would promise

to spend every waking moment propounding violence,
and I would dismiss him from my fury. First and foremost
he should renounce the Lord and all of his laws. Next, he would curse

the Lord to his face, and write an absolute firm chit
of his soul to the devil, or my brother. Without condition. Thirdly,
he should pray to God for never a moment of mercy.

Before I could finish proclaiming my articles,
Dubois started uttering litanies and blasphemies
I'm sure had never been evoked on earth prior.

My eyes teared. My shanks quivered. Neck hair stood upright
at the power he summoned while insulting our Maker.
So zealously he condemned our holy scriptures,

I'm surprised Satan himself didn't appear, to join in
or recruit him early for the infernal choirs.
Faintly, Dubois pricked his thumb. With flowing blood,

he wrote a detailed obligation of his soul to hell.
Dropping to his knees, he prayed, earnestly, for no
forgiveness, as long as the word *Jesus* survived.

Me, pleased at the efforts of these ceremonies,
ordered him to open his mouth in a widened gape
and without further ado shot him full through the throat.

So quickly I ridded of him, he could never repent,
his body a moose's gut-puddle, a miscarry
steaming, while the devil collected his due.

How thoroughly I, Cutwolfe, revenged myself on Dubois,
our jealous Lord may hold some envy for me.
And you, kindred of his, I spit in all your faces.'

The hatchet-man required no further prodding.
With his first swipes he cracked open Cutwolfe's collarbones.
Someone twisted a claw hammer into both his ears,

and with pruning shears they lobbed off each of his fingers
before working with an axe to remove his tongue and jaws.
They left him there, lashed to the lawnchair, to ponder

how one murder births another and another, and never
has bloodshed been removed from the surface of our world.
I witnessed this myself, spying one night in a rail shed.

(Th. Nashe)

For Frogs Massacred at Overwater

Why vex when they massacred frogs?
Mostly a campaign of baneful kids

and a carbon-handled medical scalpel,
skinning them alive by Overwater Bog.

Down municipal side roads, in the damp
and ditchgrass, bewildering afternoon

to duck the gutted, twitching frog flung
at my head to the merriment of others.

Why Grant, star centre of the Saint B Saints,
livened in that frog torture doled out

by that *bandito* clan of headbangers on Wite-Out?
A Peugeot bike they pedalled in the air,

lowered it onto a frog, stuck to the muck with sticks,
and marvelled at the skin of the back split, spitting

entrails clear as *Malleus Maleficarum* –
how could one retching boy stop them?

Later the victim frog, wilder the cruelty. Thinner frogs
struggled for escape; fatter ones stayed beating still

as they were spiked down onto the rocks
or punted repeatedly into the air.

More goop than blood, mucus, stringy. Already I knew
amphibians were endangered.

I'm lucky I didn't kill one of the torturers. I considered
one railroad spike to Skippy Anderson's head.

Bless you, Ms. White, my Grade 9 English teacher,
who supported Misty's petition

to not dissect a frog: with a Led Zeppelin pin they poked
white rubbery frog torso searching for seeds of heart –

now what do you think of this? Vacuous construction workers,
fathers, lifeless divorcées, alcoholics, suicides, I'm not surprised,
may your hex live on for three more of your generations.

Mooncurser, c. a Link-boy, or one who under Colour of lighting Men, Robs, them or leads them to a gang of Rogues, that will do it for him.

To Madame Justice, for Forgiveness

'Two former Mounties were charged with assaulting
city cops by tossing vegetables at them from a nineteenth
floor balcony. David and Daniel D— pretended to sleep
in the same bed when cops came to arrest them…'
                                    – *Winnipeg Sun*

I was stationed for twenty years with the RCMP
at Innu Reservation. Each day I drank alone
or with my wife. The most fun we ever had was when
she would plastic-jug up batches of homemade wine.

She'd brew chokecherries, dandelions, raspberries –
whatever she'd get her hands on, actually;
it was tough for her right from the start, came she couldn't
pump gas without getting harassed for her blue eyes.

Each November I dreaded driving around town
blowing away dogs, but it was part of the job.
Once I came across a toddler mauled to shreds
in the schoolyard. I couldn't spend a day fishing

without looking over my back. Other than drinking,
the only fun we had at night was smooching in the bath.
Ever walk in a house where the plumbing stays frozen
for months? Those people whiz through a hole in the floor

right into their basements. It's young and old people
who have it toughest. The worst part is home visits,
to drag kids to class, and seeing a girl without clothes
passed out on the floor beside an uncle or coz.

After some years of this she left me – eventually,
Madame Justice, I was stationed back in the city.
My name's Dave D— and I threw rutabaga
with my brother off my ex's balcony. Forgive me.

Mayor Sam Katz and Star Chamber

Whom do you plumb with your gasser tongue?
It's no knee-slapper to laugh at yourself so,
sticking out your gauche belly, laughing as you preside
over your cult of coyotes and wolves.

No one needs your craven shareholder call
for the spirituality of matter, for rebuses
and abutments of material space. You fail
to see our three fires for SOS!

When eating spaghetti on toast, wine-drunk
like the grifter I am, I'll spew laughter to hear
you died, conk-out rat you are, your yellow eyes
facing the asphalt gooey with dusk heat.

Whisky-Jack Preaches to the Wolves

Wily One, Whisky-Jack, incurred great debt, but not one fur
to sell to the traders. Over their barrels they would not give cash.
One day Whisky-Jack was as poor as a widow without sons,
so I can't say as to why they loaned him a flintlock,
two blankets, two pair of breeches, and a bag of flour.

By travois he dragged these to his wife. Naked she sat
at a cold hearth, saying, 'Wise Whisky-Jack, you spread miraculous joy
on this miserable earth, but we've no way to repay this – plus, credit
is the scam that starved us from the start.' He grinned,
'I'm off to the fort, Old Woman, to see traders again.'

Some traders thought he came to repay. 'Nope,' said Whisky-Jack.
He told one trader his nose looked crooked, so I can't say as to why
they loaned him a tin of poison. With help from his wife,
Whisky-Jack stirred the poison into a cauldron of fat.
After it hardened, they cut the mix as tiny pellets.

He brought the pellets in a bucket to the forest
with the idea of talking to some wolves. 'Hello! My friend!'
he called to one, but the wolf saw himself skinned of his pelt.
'Nope,' said Whisky-Jack, 'I wish to employ you. I offer you work,
special work, going around summoning all the wolves and foxes.

I'll sit on this perch ready to preach, to tell of good tidings.'
So that wolf went to work, telling the handsome wolves and foxes
to circle Whisky-Jack exactly as if he were a priest.
'Friends,' said Whisky-Jack, 'the tidings you hear you should accept,
then no one will ever kill you, if you take on religion.

But if you don't truly believe, someone will kill you. These pellets,
if you eat these, which I place in your teeth, you'll live on forever.'
'Let us!' wolves and foxes yelped. 'We want to live that long!'
Whisky-Jack dropped a black pellet in each mouth. 'Long shall you live,'
he said. 'Now that you've accepted this faith, you'll know peace.'

Whisky-Jack laughed as the wolves and foxes jumped in the air
and fell down dead. He scalped their pelts and carried them home,
impressed that by instructing religion he could kill so many
and in this manner pay off the great debts he had incurred.
He even repaid the traders by deceiving others with words.

Hudson's Bay Archives

Woebegone
whole generations
parsed together
in Grandma's
smirched grimace,
winter is head

warlord
in this turf war.
Double-hooded
corner sentry
is blood hosed
from sidewalk snow.

Your lit Zippo
left at the toe
of Louis Riel's
shoreline statue
cannot reclaim
sacred land.

Triangulate
us on a map
in an archive
at an outpost
trader's museum,
we sons of whoresons,

spreading sorrow
through ourselves,
and self-inflicted
crisis arousal
married with
survivor's guilt.

St. John's Avenue

The kids hunch in a circle at a coffee table
with the rue, henbane, nightshade, and thornapple
suggested in the *Ars Goetia*, distilled
into the chalice of an infernal glass pipe.

In the kitchen towers the captain of a biker gang,
with a pistol unsheathed from holster in one hand.
A kitten with mouth rot raised in his other hand,
he sacrifices to two frothing black mutts

that rend the limbs apart with snarling in seconds.
The kids, wired on vids and the black-sant
rapping from sub-woofers, flash gang signs
and goat horns at a strobe in sacrilegious thrill.

No longer an old Protestant parish under witch judge,
but these hell-crazed neighbourhoods and the kids,
the kids possessed with Luciferian whim,
while hags with sick babes in the basement hide.

Red Riding Hood

He never summoned Cthulhu for courage before.
The timeworn hound in the parents' backyard never really tried
running down a hare. The bird was carved and put away.

Stuffed and dozed, dishwater hanging a warm steam
behind the curtains while he laced on his boots,
not really certain what was inspiring him, unmasked

by the frost and piercing down to roots. Knee-high drifts,
and night became years when he wouldn't call,
when distance felt invincible under a low violet wash.

But tonight, with Canis raising, he's palming his cell to call,
and can already tell, he's talking with her sister, only to be told
she married a doctor and moved to Melbourne.

Tracked out to a field challenging the indomitable sum
of wind chill, what made him hang up without another word?
Some things can't be planned for or recovered from.

Chief Peguis Trail

Not without crossing a striker part of town,
not without trash-barrel fires scenting my coat,
not without carrying a garrotte in my palm

in case death tries to halt me from your lips.
A street-level dealer offers me a boost,
a child berates me for any bits of change,

my flesh navigates these parapets of space,
traversing this interval away from you.
Always there exists this distance with us,

as I pass the wilds of the Crown land
and cross the cement bridge at the river's curve
for the walkway into the urban reserve.

Outside Lanigan

This hulking grain silo feels reverent in the full moon,
our sanctum of steel beam, batten, corrugated iron
that shifts with movements of wind off our candle flame.
We had passed the Town of Lanigan, following faded
highway paint, wired but giddy with love, while distant
farmhouse granges formed ahead like crumbled bookends.

You, my love, suggested we follow fields left fallow,
then led us waist-deep through a tract of ripening mustard,
but I was the one that kissed you at the silver maple
and saw the pegboard cola sign pitched against the barn.
And, there, a derelict baler with orange moon above
embellished one grain silo with rusted door ajar.

What floor was once here has overgrown with thistle.
Our candle whispers as we read Sir Philip Sydney,
To the Countess of Pembroke's Arcadia, the chapter
where fishermen find a shepherd washed up on the shore,
as I watch you scissor one leg into your turquoise garter
so our imprint will remain tomorrow when we're gone.

Rider Boys

Gup, Rider,
wily cur
son of a burr-
bushed witch
with bramble itch
in the armpit
of the continent,
your green
real obscene
on Labour Day.
Of all prairie
Commonwealth cities
named for queens,
none as foul,
strankly, spleen-
smelling as dour
Regina – trees
scrawny, dead
bespectacled tellers,
juice-harpers,
truck customizers
whose wives creak
as wheat elevators,
like that Lancaster,
just some lucky
mechanical
bull-rider,
son of a plucky
bingo caller
from the underworld
lost on your plains.
What rural brains
or town knave said
melons on your head

would help you win?
It's just a joke,
your goblin yoke,
to draw hornets
to your Rider stench,
it's ever your way
on Banjo Day
to block the trochee
chant starting
from the east:
'Go, Bombers, Go!'
Gup, Riders,
behold the view
the Blue reigneth
over you.

Potable

Canteens are costly. Gatorade
bottles can be pulled from any bin.
They never leak. If you bash them,
they never stay misshapen.
Dehydration means dead.
Joint pain, overeating, swooning,
lagging pep, lest your slumming
desires these effects, a third of walkabouts,
don't forget, should entail scrounging
for potable water. Every house, a hose.
Espy, if you're forced, until a bootleg
to a tap clears. Hide in a trash barrel,
or the ribs of an upturned canoe. Once
I lurked in a development for weeks,
slaking thirst, gorging snow peas,
pod and all. Wherever water pools,
provided you've procured iodine pills,
consider a source: motor oil pans,
discarded sports helmets, community
swimming holes, or dips in eaves
of roofs are known to hold a lick,
if you're the type to scale a fire escape
for a snooze. You can always pinch
some later from a fountain in a mall,
but recall the medieval proverb
from when we owned little more
than parched flesh: don't dare toss
dirty water until you find fresh.

Nip, c. a Cheat; also to Pinch or Sharp any thing. Nip a bung, c. to cut a Purse. To Nip, to Press between the Fingers and Thumb without the Nails, or with any broad Instrument like a pair of Tongs as to squeeze between Edged Instruments or Pincers.

Residential Shack Resort

This city is a contrast between our beat-to-hell
and our beautiful Dollarstores. While I strive today
in the parkway behind St. John's Avenue,
who knew this shack resort is where I'd stay?

I thank this gang war for boasting beautiful soldiers.
But you, Tina, suppose I'll just pay my taxes, eat fried-
egg sandwiches, pull out the burr, bramble, twigs, and fern
from my hair? You suppose this: inside my shack

I'll assemble a canopy bed frame in the corner
when a mattress on the floor proves sufficient? I saw this
in childhood, clear to the lane trash bins, and can't forget
the piss-eyed bull mastiff who hung himself

over the neighbour's snow fence. I promise you my grief
shall gather mass, like the rotting hiss of burn-off flares
above the gas plants and steel mills. I know your commands
and harsh confidence: you're beautiful, yes, but love is

a legless beggar scooching on a wheeled plank,
never smiling unless fortune caresses the cup.
You suppose I'll try a break-and-enter, make rent
selling hot guitars at country-and-western bars

at Higgins and Main? You suppose I'll get pulled over
on parole in a stolen Mustang to see an old bro
in Fort Saskatchewan? Nothing of me deduces
easy, Tina, I'm a dark thin man with high cheekbones

on long-term disability from the boot factory.
We both attended dysfunctional school systems,
and we both wonder what is wrong with this. Where
was the smell of torched garages, I smell wet cement.

Runner Song

She notes a hex in the parkade;
by dark she fears the boogeyman;
her brother's ghost may never fade
where black-clad hoods caught up to him.
She blesses bannock with a hymn
now her ex is free on bail;
I'll measure fortune by my blade,
in every house the witch's wail.

She sprinkles brick dust out the door;
we stay clear of poems by Villon;
we cuddle and fuck on the floor,
lest gunshots through the window come;
it could be her ex or his chum
who bangs a board with crooked nail,
but by my blade I'll settle score,
in every house the witch's wail.

Kids Learn About Secret Members

Shoebox colonies butted side by side. Old HVAC
of electric baseboards patched together
like burning barrels star-charting our backyards.
Our kids disassemble so subtly these days,

not only to drive-bys, but to Mallarmé's image of swans
frozen in ice. The insolence and the insouciance,
our kids won't adopt older patterns, conditioned
by cut-ups, never at their strived-for best.

They're syringe needles rolling under
beds; they're leather breeches hanging off worn slacks;
they're the prickly pink, stubbled, pimply, shaved pubis
beneath the tassel fringe on a short dress, that bad.

Our kids inhabit unreachable depths, yet,
at times, they can surprise as a whole town
can march behind the hockey sticks.
Commend our kids, how some will always love

and some will always lust, and some will sample all
kinds, and some will dare discuss the sentience
of Jainism at a Mennonite pig roast. Commend,
some will transcend the greige on travel points

to English Guyana, perhaps, pivoting the tabletop
down from the cold north, from Uncle Ron Demarski's
camo-netted moonshine still on his back lot,
to equatorial poets, turquoise. Commend,

when our kids make it to a zinc countertop,
a little fazed from a rum hut, tossing candy corn
into the hoops of their gulping greedy mouths.
While a horny TV evangelical from the nineties

informs about the Movement of Secret Members.
About mostly pornography. Like how the iguana sunning
in a palm tree signifies the grand lizard reset
and main Reptilian way of enslaving our colony.

At Her Flint Cottage

Putting away a lover's cutlery at her flint cottage
in the sticks, in the sticks of the sticks, she stretches
in amiable peace beside a woodstove red-berried

with heat, as she searches pages in a pulp fantasy
that had sat in a cupboard since the Raëlian Happenings.
Likely the dirtiest Tor book for a decade, the kind

a frizzy-haired motorcycle mama really enjoyed
while wearing a muumuu beside a filling bathtub.
My lover left it earmarked to later read aloud,

to imbue us with blue, like last night when we heard
about the Black Mountain Ozark orgy hiked upon
by some high-school graduates from San Fran.

Tonight's the night I quit the artifice-stabilizers,
I decide, as we trek a cold white beach line,
in scratchy wools to heighten our sensations,

our arms bitten, bleeding through our tweeds, by horseflies
cycling above crabgrass. This is what I need, sweat at last
to purge me of poems by Giacomo Leopardi.

This is my petition to a full moon answered,
to get led away from the fossilized car parkades
in the convalescing balm of a cloven-heeled girl.

Salt

It's not because of dogged sadness alone
that you draw a bath, crook back your neck,
let the grain of your face unpattern,
but it is because it is maniacal

glee to liberate the battered body
from the tenterhooks of poorly ironed clothes,
to drown with books and what whisperings

emitting off the day, and lie and feel
the tympanum of washroom waterworks
chant your name in the unctuous broil.

To slide away from your apricating,
you'll dissolve your bones until they're vinegary,
or what you pray is you'll allow the fireweed
of your nerves to dissolve into Epsom.

Tribe of Bens

> 'Sir, if you be not the quiet the quicklier, I'll ha' you
> clapp'd fairly by the heels, for disturbing the Fair.'
> — *Bartholomew Fair*, B. Jonson

A Falmouth import of a track star,
Ben, fastest anabolic Canadian,
techno-legging a 100m to snatch gold.
A steely Bardolf below the din,
Ben, the beer belly and *Exergasia*
levelled in one, so big a nose
and a brain, he may've caught it
in an epigram: what wyrd fortune in a name
to mint one with another man.

Prig-napper, c. the Sixth Order of the Canting Crew, Horse Stealers, who carry a Bridle in their Pockets, a small Pad Saddle in their Breeches.

Archived

VHS dubbed from my summer tweens, I untrunk
after years pent to the plunk of my thirtieth
at the Golden Rim Motor Inn. That vid I clunk

in the slit, stick the empty play button with ballpoint pen,
finger fast forward to the final climax
of *Jason and the Argonauts*. Just as the Colchian king,

Aeëtes, from handfuls of Hydra's teeth out his helmet,
evokes six ranks of skeletons. They thrust up from sunbaked fields
with jawbones shrieking wind, and as a spear rings off a shield

and Medea slumps, dead for the moment, the screen hisses,
morphs as rainbow-coloured bars to Captain Barney Miller.
Brown brogues braced on his oak desk, munching on a meatloaf

sandwich, Barney dishes, 'Be polite, Kid,' to Stanley
'Wojo' Wojciehowicz, while at the far end of the set,
Fish wrangles on the phone with his wife. The audience claps,

a bass-sprung collage of credits pass. Plastic wheels squeal
and after a lull of dull white noise, I get to it:
the slow-mo epic recording of my dungeon-crawling

ninety-nine ill-lit levels of Tengen's *Gauntlet*. The eight-bit
masterpiece I caught with patch cords, output cables,
and a VCR (half pancaked by a wrestling move) in my bedroom

back in Grade 7. In my last cromlech, at my peak,
slaying Morak and the Green Dragon for the Sacred Orb.
Without as rewarding a quest completed ever since.

Fire Song

Hosanna,
as love has never uncomplicated itself,
your memories never escape their spell
of why they recount: you can't disavow
you more destroyed than built things – He-Men,
model tanks, Barbies you set on sawhorses
to film while shooting with high-powered pellets.

Hosanna,
you won't disown you scissored
each letter of Thomas Dekker's 'May-song,'
spun them in a hat with each letter
of your lover's name, to paste that one long
barbarous word on a stone church wall,
as love has never uncomplicated itself.

Hosanna,
as love has never uncomplicated itself
in your heart, so you fight
like a badger on a barbed leash, the state
that keeps you yanking, twisting
on the chain, rankling by instinct stung,
whether it's a curse to think love is foolish.

Firebugs

Fields by tracks, bins, sheds
behind a school for deaf kids –
countless edges holla to torch.

Although the mayor tried to decree
lighters safe from firebugs,
most learned to bend back the teeth

and thumb free the metal wheel.
With Mason jars of gasoline, or flame
throwers made with plumber tubing

duct-taped onto a can of Raid,
the firebug's greatest trophy remains
boarded houses set aflame.

The best comeuppance in the city,
that smoldering embryo dawn
in black smithereens of snow:

exhausted heat clinkering down
into smoot, calx, coal, and slag,
to see a square of land reclaimed.

Lilith
for Guy Maddin

Nothing spookier than the night
your internet hook-up goes home,
and you're in bed alone,
in a dream or half-dream,
lying with the window open.

When an old crone flies in,
nothing spookier than all your sins
visited upon you, and Lilith descends
through layers of covers
on her helpless victim.

Her sparkling beady eyes,
her withering touch, and some singed
banality awakening within you,
you can't decide whether seized
or savoured.

She whispers as if she reads
a folk narrative, and nothing
spookier as she embraces
the need to reconcile
both your broken histories.

Propped above the bed,
she rasps, 'You're all corrupt kids
of skin-walker descent,
and nothing will stop me
from finding you again.'

Transit Stop

A sickly citizen was taking the transit
from Cathedral, he was riding that night.

That night fortune was divined by all,
watching him shiver in the wheelchair seats.

He wore a greasy jacket that said 'Inco Mines.'
He was a dark frail skeleton in the bus glare.

He wore a turquoise bolo tie, a Gambler
Stetson, rawhide tassels, snake-skins with taps,

and down the stairs he stumbled, on Provencher,
standing with rye whisky Slurpee, thinking:

Of course his bus ride ended with a stabbing,
not a finish line, but crime scene tape.

Whip-Jacks, c. the tenth Order of the Canting Crew; Counterfeit Mariners Begging with false Passes, pretending Shipwrecks, great Losses at Sea, &c. narrow escapes; telling dismal Stories, having learnt Tar-terms on purpose, but are meer Cheats.

What Am I?

Iron ramrod.
Resurrected
from a high school
recycle bin.
Braced and filed
by black goggles
on a six-foot lathe.
Tinder-sparked off
a six-point file.
Tip pounded by
ball-peen hammer
on an anvil.
Spit on, papered.
Oiled, sheened.
Handle wound
with rubbery bands
of electrical tape.
Worn into grooves
of a fierce grip.
Weighted perfect
at centre-point
on the thumb tip
of a burnout
bass guitarist
in advanced class.
Giggling endorsed
in the palms of six.
Tested, stabbed,
scalped the red vinyl
skin off a binder
for Language Arts.
Smuggled out
in the hollow cover
of a Social Studies

text. Stashed under
a brown Firebird's
passenger seat,
parked in the front
of a Night Owl
on Aberdeen Street.
A short kid who studies
hard, one day dreams
to teach gym. Hidden up
a hoodie sleeve.

When Whisky-Jack Didn't Want To Heal

> 'Brightness falls from the air;
> Queens have died, young and fair;
> Lord have mercy upon us.'
> – Thomas Nashe

Whisky-Jack was as ever hungry and alone, this is a sacred song
I try to sing, that he flew north wanting to heal his hurt heart.
The deer path he followed ended, the bog lumpen with great stones ended,
and past the tree line he landed in the high North. His lungs emptied –
  this place

had no black pine branches for him to land on – so Whisky-Jack slept
in a gusset of speargrass, knowing it not safe on the open earth.
He dove into dreamtime: he remembered an alphabet in the trees
he flew in, he remembered the daughter of a Willow Goddess

who briefly tamed him – but Whisky-Jack didn't see the bear
out of the shadows sneaking! The bear, with his long middle claw,
tickled Whisky-Jack's shiny black head. Bear said, 'I am Jacob Boehme,
old doctor, old poisioner. Little Grey Jay, you've flown far from home,

your loved ones worry. Whether it be a furry tongue from an adder's bite,
gut-rot from fangs of a skipe, or heart-knock conditioned at the touch
of a horned toad, all antidote exists in the venom, and the black vile
oozing from out your glans – you can refine it into gold only if you return

to your loved ones.' Whisky-Jack's heart beat in terror, his eyes bridled
with icicles. He flew further north, to where the stars glowed inside
an aureate-froze sea, and he landed and fell into a deep sleep.
Jackrabbit hopped up to Whisky-Jack. Jackrabbit said, 'I am Paracelsus,

student of Johannes Trithemius, the great abbot of St. James
in Würzburg, Bavaria. I can tell you that to make a friend, get a bag,
put a sturgeon's bones inside, sneak a tail feather from Thunderbird's nest,
and bury these items in a ground oven lit from the sparking flint

off a caribou's rutting hoof. Let the substrate bake for forty days,
and you can call it (after it hatches) a homunculus. Take great care,
afterwards you can teach it the names of things, and if you're patient,
and it's clever, it can teach itself to create others of its kind.

Soon you'll know many, many friends.' Whisky-Jack didn't understand -
he only wanted to make a willow branch into a spear, and he flew far north
to where constellations rotated on all sides. He didn't know if he was awake
or asleep. He heard a voice. 'You have to leave the North, Whisky-Jack.'

He saw it was Grandmother Fox – she almost touched her snout to his beak!
He felt the bones in his wings tingling to where his heart beat
before an egg of ambrosial warmth surrounded him. A boiling heat
radiated on him from above – he felt his body rotting into putrid black

before transforming into a rosy perfection brighter than Thunderbird's wings.
This terrified Whisky-Jack and he started flying. 'I am Thomas Rawlins,'
he heard Grandmother Fox speak. 'You have to leave the North to heal,
Whisky-Jack. All things from one and to one, in the centre, truth,

at the circumference, vanity, and your loved ones are waiting for you at
    your home.'
But Whisky-Jack had already started flying back toward the South. He
    cried while flying.
Where fell his tears gooseberries sprouted from the earth, and this is the end
of the sacred story I tried to sing, of how Whisky-Jack didn't want to heal
    his hurt heart.

Plains Ballad

Stargazing on the beach in Scanterbury
I'm a poorly piper among the Cree,
my heart inclined to Elizabeth,
light of my dreams and life of my breath.

Mornings she arrives from the east on her steed,
her father beside her proclaiming the deed.
Her bust as pale white as the frosty plain;
if I thought she loved me it would heal my pain.

When I trill like a whisky-jack for her applause
her father accuses me of lacking a cause,
but the look in her eyes if I start to jig
enrages him enough to call me a Whig.

He calls me a knave if I kick up my heels,
but that's how I roll if the fiddler runs reels.
He reminds me his daughter is married by rote,
then says trade my tassels for a red coat.

When she married a corporal in the RCMP,
John A. Macdonald proclaimed the decree:
cursed are the Métis and the adoptee.
I whoop with an uncle at the passing train;
if I thought she loved me it would heal my pain.

At Logan and Keewatin

All along these concrete crumpled streets,
like talons from the curb, rebar bursts
where the alley ends. Where upturned trash bins
stack up amid mouldering chesterfields,
the strip mall stillwaters within
murky windows: all edges waver together
with the torque of corrosion and ruin porn.
Yet the best parts are to see the lots
turned to swamps at the rush of nature:
cubed cars, crushed as bales, wall in the mill,
and these wild graffiti, we should think,
sprayed on the rusty ribs of a train bridge,
are doom-laden runic above the land-lock
of our golden plain pulverized to chalk.
Yet let us protect this from the pollsters
for renewal, those glib revitalizers
not for the unhinging of infrastructure,
who discourage the squatters for scorning
a bank card, who encourage the talkers
toward a garble of assessments.
There would exist no junk heap for old dogs
to die under, no crane boom suspended,
like a crepitating palsied finger
or sprite chimera over the shoulder.
To spiffy this up would belittle the point
of your absence. By a lingering presence,
I'll remember and I'll dissemble you
in the sheets of scrap metal warped by time,
your palm deep in the elemental grain.

Letter to Leonard Peltier

It's true, Leonard, construction workers dig up the bones
of your ancestors, voices in the river scream
through turbines, and not hymnals, native mysticism,
nor medical science could save your Nookum

on life support. The burning spoor of cancer
is through her now. Fuck the muthafuckers.
Fuck us, too, we've lost track of all land settlement claims
and are the wheels and pulleys of wastewater plants.

It's a miracle when your grandson plays the drum.
This spring I've yet to hear of a screwdriver stabbing,
firebombing, suicide, or elder abuse.
The moccasins I've traded in for a pair of steel toes

to take a full-time position at a potash mine.
My shift exists at the perimeter of the fence,
but the powwow taught me love is a counter-script.
I'm deeply sorry about your Nookum, Leonard.

Did you kill any agents? If you even did, we forgive
as we need you walking the Red Road to heal.
Lakota, fly your flag at the edge of the oilfield
and I heard, till this day, elders are uncontacted still

with pockets of tribes who refuse to trade.
The weather is hot on the north-central plains.
I'm still in love, Leonard, but starting to witness how
there's barely a difference between savage and saved.

I'm sure you heard – we lost the swamplands to liars,
molesters, lords. As for me, I should've known
I'd never find love's bullion in bankrupt concrete.
And I'm travelling to Pine Ridge by way of Batoche.

The meaning of *Cree* is cry, scream, call, shout,
shriek, yell, holler, whoop, squawk, screech, wail, weep;
and everything I see is enemy to your dream.
This is the final letter I can write you, Leonard.

Go Long, Boys

At last our raider caravan clears
Skull Pan Pond for the flatland,
a Starseed on our radar. Our radium
crosshairs dead-centre, and, as happens,
Prince's *1999* from Pointman's feed.
Go long, boys.

At dawn we sight a small red gourd
with legendary seed off our flank side,
as livening as chokecherry scruff
at the bend in Red River bluff,
with pith that invigorates the mind.
Go long, boys.

The swim-up bar with Tina, away at last.
Whether there hides some poet's occultism
in Apuleius's *Golden Ass*,
is the afternoon's fool's errand.
As crayfish boil over caesium-blue flame,
and white egrets breast searing blades of sun.
Go long, boys.

Notes

Night Became Years juxtaposes contemporary, urban vocabulary with archaic canting language, a secret dialect of the underclasses in Elizabethan England. Cant was developed through the collision and fission of cultures in Europe over 400 years ago; speculation is that it derives primarily from the peoples of Romany, the 'gypsies,' who – much like Métis peoples spread across North America – propel toward cultural definition within other entrenched cultures, over vast geographic expanses.

There is value, I believe, in looking at historical communities, like the outsider and criminal classes of Elizabethan times, to observe how these definitions relate, differ from, and inform our neighbourhoods of today. Today I see canting terms in the vitality of hip-hop, whether in dis songs, ride songs, or in the personae and forms artists adopt to tell their stories; I appreciate the creative and confrontational wordplay in inner-city environments as developing narrative for different classes, and evidence that the terms we use to define ourselves can both liberate and shackle us and our communities.

In my own life, I often consider how the diverse aspects of my biological history (Métis), my familial heritage (adoptee), and my immediate environment (Winnipeg) fuse in my poetry. Calling myself a Métis adoptee from Winnipeg feels reductive, or presumptuous, or disrespectful of my family, even though this is how the Adoption Unit of Aboriginal and Northern Affairs has defined me. For perhaps to exist amid the frayed cables of diverse backgrounds is no culture whatsoever – but perhaps it's something new and liberating. Because, at last, historically and into the future, for any adoptee, for an immigrant, for any wanderer of fortune desiring definition, individuality solidifies by what of our selves we choose to embrace, erase, or revise.

Throughout the book there are repeated references to the Elizabethan poet and pamphleteer Thomas Nashe. Little is known of Nashe's background, but it is evident that he was a rabble-rouser; he was once imprisoned with the great poet and playwright Ben Jonson for their collaborative satirical play, *Isle of Dogs*. Nashe continually confronted his environment with violent, railing, original, and brilliant wordplay. Not unlike the hero of his picturesque ribald novel, Jack Wilton in *The Unfortunate Traveller*, Nashe cantered about England during the Black Plague while beefing with his enemies in pamphlets that showed off his wit, fiery temper, moralizing, mocking, bawdy, and original prose styling. He was one of the first writers in English to mash up High Latin and back-alley slang. There is some conjecture that Thomas Nashe was the front man for none other than Edward de Vere, who some postulate could've been Shakespeare.

The definitions of canting terms on pages 7, 8, 14, 23, 32, 40, 56, 69, 77, and 83 are from *The First English Dictionary of Slang, 1699* (Bodleian Library University of Oxford, 2010), which is a modern version of *A New Dictionary of the Terms Ancient and Modern of the Canting Crew, In its Several Tribes, of Gypsies, Beggers, Thieves, Cheats, &c.* by B. E. Gent, 1699.

p. 17, twenty-sided die: common polyhedral die for playing role-playing games.

p. 33, Moody and Sankey: *Sacred Songs and Solos*, 1877. Popular hymn collection.

p. 33, Waldensians: also Vaudois, a Pre-Protestant Christian movement, persecuted by Catholics, see Milton's 'On the Late Massacre in Piedmont.'

p. 34, 'Night Skating' is based on a poem by Eugenio Montale.

p. 42, Matthew Arnold: 1822–1888. English poet and inspector of schools.

p. 47, Marina Tsvetaeva: 1892–1941. Icon, Russian poet, persecuted under the regime of Stalinist Soviet Union.

pp. 48–53, 'Cutwolfe,' for readers unaware, is recut from a section of Thomas Nashe's *Unfortunate Traveller*. Readers are encouraged to seek out the original text, in both Penguin Editions and the public domain.

p. 54, *Malleus Maleficarum*: 1487–present. Inquisitor treatise on trying and persecuting witches and suspected witches.

pp. 59–60, Whisky-Jack: or grey jay, a plucky little resilient bird, Canada's contested national bird, a winter survivor in the coldest climes. Called *Wisakêcâhk* in Cree, it's a complicated trickster bird in North American Plains Indigenous mythology. This particular myth is reconstructed from a story transcribed in *Sacred Stories of the Sweet Grass Cree*, published for schoolchildren in 1928 by Canada's Department of Mines.

p. 62, *Ars Goetia*, the Lesser Key of Solomon: anonymous grimoire, circa 1600s, compiled over several centuries.

p. 63, Cthulhu: from Lovecraftian mythos, a gigantic octopus entity believed to have control over people's minds.

p. 65, Sir Philip Sydney, 1554–1586. Elizabethan-era courtier, soldier, poet and defender of poetics, noted for his early serial prose novel, *Arcady*, as well as his pimples, sonnets, courage, and early death.

p. 66, Gup: obsolete term, used to express derision.

p. 71, François Villon: 1431–1463. French poet renowned for celebrating the criminal underworld in his works, a ruffian and jailbird who adopted his stepfather's name.

p. 72, Stéphane Mallarmé: 1842–1898. French Symbolist poet.

p. 73, Reptilians, or lizard people. A purported race of reptile humanoids, often referenced in science fiction, fantasy, and conspiracy theories – or some sort of master race that controls peoplekind from subterranean caverns.

p. 74, Raëlians; Raëlism. 1974–present. UFO religion founded by ex-sportscar journalist Claude Vorilhon. Did he choose this name because of the sound proximity to Louis Riel and his movement?

p. 74, Giacomo Leopardi: 1798 –1837. Italian philosopher, poet, essayist, and noted philologist.

p. 76, Tribe of Ben, or Sons of Ben. SOB were dramatists influenced by Jonson's drama; TOB were Cavalier poets, like Herrick, and Lovelace, and Suckling, and Carew, influenced by Jonson's poetry. Followers gathered at the Devil's Tavern to get merry with Good Ben and follow his rules of Conviviality, a celebration of the friendly and lively. Also, Jonson is a noted Epigramist and writer of songs and Royal Masques.

p. 76, Bardolph: Postulated as a caricature of Ben Jonson, the generational barkeep of Falstaff and Hal's merry crew.

p. 76, Exergasia: rhetorical term, from Latin, The Gorgeous, the final and perhaps penultimate style according to George Puttenhams's *Arte of English Posey*, a book that Ben Jonson considered so important he guarded it from others.

p. 78, Aeëtes, in Greek myth, the son of the sun and ocean. Medea, his daughter, stole away with Jason and the Argo after he and his Argonauts retrieved the Golden Fleece.

p. 78, *Gauntlet*, 1985: hack-and-slash dungeon-crawling role-playing game, originally arcade platformer but famous on the basic Nintendo Entertainment System.

p. 79, 'Rankling with instinct stung,' in 'Fire Song,' is Shakespeare.

p. 79, 'May-song': Thomas Dekker, 1572–1632.

p. 81, Lilith, from Babylonian, Jewish, and Biblical texts, the mother of all succubi or night-hags.

p. 81, Skin-walkers: from Navajo myth. In most stories, skin-walkers and humans are in a battle for life or death.

pp. 86–87, The myth of Whisky-Jack (*Wîsakêcâhk: wîsakê*, to hurt, and *acâhk*, soul, spirit) flying to the North to heal his heart is an imagined one. Marrying Whisky-Jack, a traditional Indigenous trickster character, with Christian esoteric mysticism is my attempt to reconcile elements of my own mixed heritage.

p. 86, Jacob Boehme: 1575–1624. Lutheran mystic philosopher.

p. 86, Paracelsus: 1493–1541. Swiss physician, alchemist, astrologer, and magician of the German Renaissance.

p. 87, Thomas Rawlins: 1620?–1670. Alchemist, English poet.

p. 89, 'At Logan and Keewatin' is owed to works of the poet Richard Hugo. His 'In Stafford Country' was the jump-off point for my poem.

pp. 90–91, Leonard Peltier, 1944–. Convicted, perhaps unjustly, in the 1970s of murder at Pine Ridge Reservation, and serving two life sentences, under sometimes harsh conditions, and yet despite public outcry, no president has been willing to pardon Leonard.

p. 92, Apuleius's *Golden Ass*: the Latin novel is sometimes seen as an allegory, with Lucius's journey as an ass exhorting readers to refrain from strong self-will and inordinate levels of curiosity lest they tangle with Fortune and plunge themselves into danger and despair.

Acknowledgments

I need to acknowledge artistic debt to Winnipeg's early and various hip-hop scene, especially at the early millennium: John Smith, Brooklyn (Rest In Peace), Ladee Seduction, John C., Wab Kinew, and a number of other artists on record labels Peanuts and Corn and Heatbag Records always inspired me to look freshly at our turf.

I also lift my glass in sincere thanks to Leslie Mundwiler (Rest In Peace), the poet and proprietor of Highbrow Books, at a windy corner of the core, who enriched me with the Elizabethan texts that inform this book.

A special thank you to program staff for allowing me to discuss poetry with prisoners at Stony Mountain Penitentiary, and especially inmates Jason and Jason, who provided the impetus for me to write 'Letter to Leonard Peltier.'

A number of these poems have appeared in various publications including *ARC, Prairie Fire, Grain, Nashwaak Review, CV2, Misunderstandings Magazine, Tart, The Winnipeg Free Press*, and *Hacksaw* magazine. Thank you to the editors. Special thank you to Andris Taskans, senior editor of *Prairie Fire*, and judge Ken Babstock, for presenting me with the Bliss Carmen Award for Poetry, for 'Letter to Leonard Peltier.'

Sincere gratitude to August Kleinzahler and John Burnside for considerate correspondence and blurbing this book. Most thanks to my brilliant and patient editor, Jeramy Dodds, brilliant and tireless Alana Wilcox, and Coach House Books. Thanks to Greg Younging and Neal McLeod for counsel. My indebtedness to Dave and Dayna. Thank you, Shayna, for clerical support. Special thanks to the Banff Centre for the Arts and Creativity, where a number of these poems were written or revised.

All love to my collaborator, Ruby, and my daughters, Jessica and Gracie. This book is dedicated to my mother and father, and sister, Jennifer, for all your love and guidance.

Jason Stefanik proudly resides in Winnipeg's spirited North End. A poet, second-generation adoptee, and recipient of the Bliss Carmen Award for Poetry, he likes to spend his time reading and writing poetry.

Typeset in Caslon

Printed at the Coach House on bpNichol Lane in Toronto, Ontario, on
Zephyr Antique Laid paper, which was manufactured, acid-free, in Saint-
Jérôme, Quebec, from second-growth forests. This book was printed with
vegetable-based ink on a 1973 Heidelberg KORD offset litho press. Its
pages were folded on a Baumfolder, gathered by hand, bound on a Sulby
Auto-Minabinda and trimmed on a Polar single-knife cutter.

Designed by Alana Wilcox
Cover art, *Red Riding Hood*, by Matt Cunningham
Author photo by Elise Nadeau

Coach House Books
80 bpNichol Lane
Toronto ON M5S 3J4
Canada

416 979 2217
800 367 6360

mail@chbooks.com
www.chbooks.com